My Emotions
Mes émotions

SCARED
LA PEUR

A Crabtree Roots Book
Un livre de la collection Les racines de Crabtree

Written by/Autrice:
Amy Culliford

Crabtree Publishing
crabtreebooks.com

School-to-Home Support for Caregivers and Teachers

This book helps children grow by letting them practice reading. Here are a few guiding questions to help the reader with building his or her comprehension skills. Possible answers appear here in red.

Before Reading:

- What do I think this book is about?
    - *This book is about feeling scared.*
    - *This book is about what feeling scared looks or feels like.*
- What do I want to learn about this topic?
    - *I want to learn what to do if I feel scared.*
    - *I want to learn what feeling scared looks like.*

During Reading:

- I wonder why...
    - *I wonder why we cry when we are scared.*
    - *I wonder why trying new things is scary.*

What have I learned so far?

- *I have learned that scared is an emotion.*
- *I have learned that some people yell when they are scared.*

After Reading:

- What details did I learn about this topic?
    - *I have learned that it is good to tell someone you are scared.*
    - *I have learned that everyone can feel scared about something.*
- Read the book again and look for the vocabulary words.
    - *I see the word **hide** on page 6 and the word **storms** on page 8. The other vocabulary words are found on page 14.*

Soutien de l'école à la maison pour les parents, les gardiens et les enseignants

Ce livre aide les enfants à se développer grâce à la pratique de la lecture. Voici quelques exemples de questions pour aider le lecteur ou la lectrice à développer ses capacités de compréhension. Les suggestions de réponses sont indiquées en rouge.

Avant la lecture

- De quoi ce livre parle-t-il?
    - *Ce livre parle du sentiment de la peur.*
    - *Ce livre explique à quoi ressemble la peur ou ce que l'on ressent.*
- Qu'est-ce que je veux apprendre sur ce sujet?
    - *Je veux apprendre quoi faire quand j'ai peur.*
    - *Je veux apprendre à quoi ressemble le sentiment de la peur.*

Pendant la lecture

- Je me demande pourquoi...
    - *Je me demande pourquoi je pleure quand j'ai peur.*
    - *Je me demande pourquoi essayer de nouvelles choses me fait peur.*
- Qu'est-ce que j'ai appris jusqu'à présent?
    - *J'ai appris que la peur est une émotion.*
    - *J'ai appris que certaines personnes crient quand elles ont peur.*

Après la lecture

- Nomme quelques détails que tu as retenus.
    - *J'ai appris que je peux dire à quelqu'un que j'ai peur.*
    - *J'ai appris que tout le monde peut avoir peur de quelque chose.*
- Lis le livre à nouveau et cherche les mots de vocabulaire.
    - *Je vois le mot **cache** à la page 6 et le mot **orages** à la page 8. Les autres mots de vocabulaire se trouvent à la page 14.*

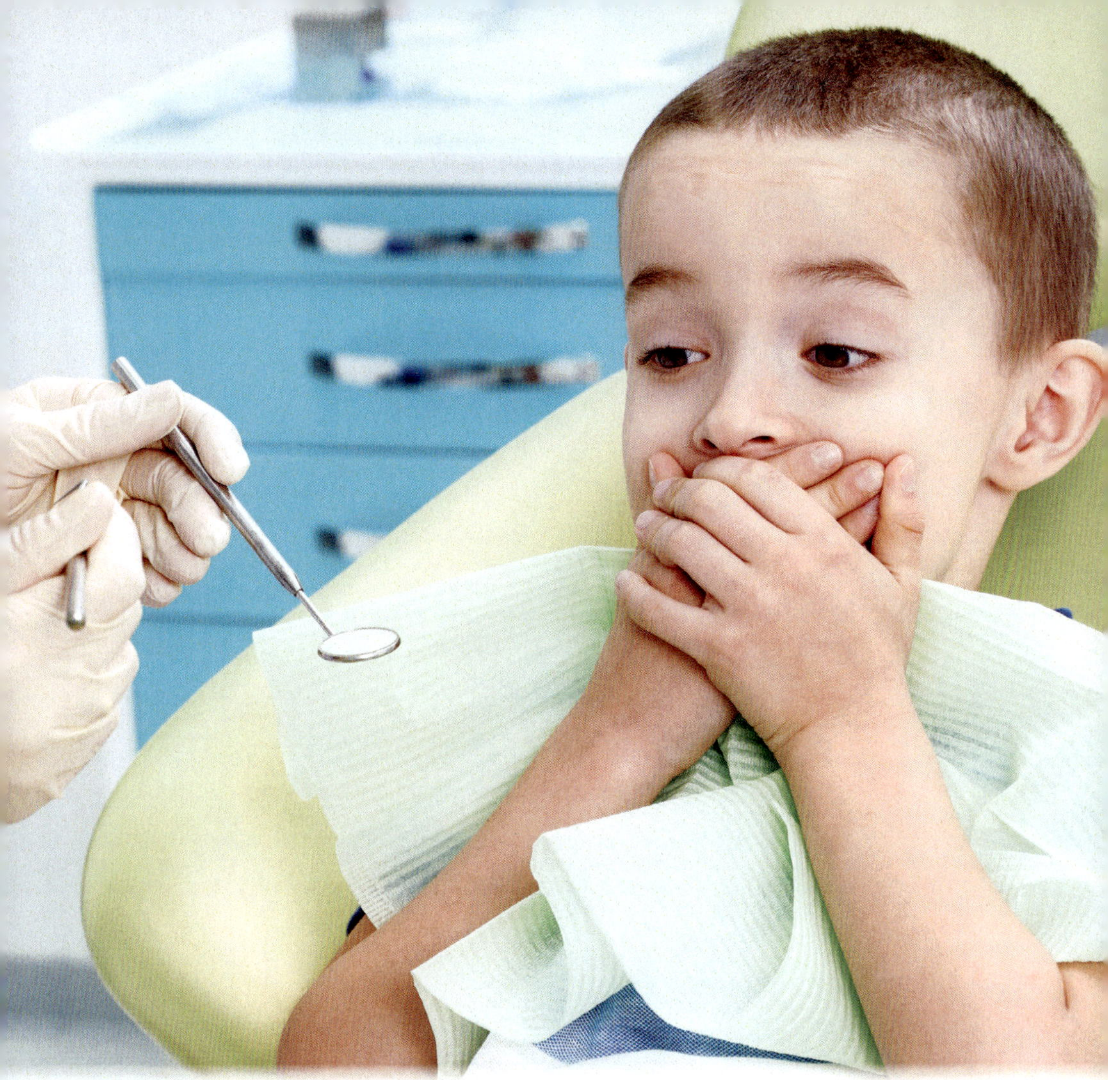

What **scares** you?

Qu’est-ce qui te fait **peur**?

I am scared of the **dark**.

J'ai peur dans le **noir**.

I **hide** when I am scared.

Je me **cache** quand j'ai peur.

I am scared of **storms**.

J'ai peur des **orages**.

I **cry** when am I am scared.

Je **pleure** quand j'ai peur.

I go find my **mom** when I am scared.

Je vais voir **maman** quand j'ai peur.

What scares you?

Qu’est-ce qui te fait peur?

Word List / Liste de mots

Sight Words / Mots courants

Sight Words		Mots courants	
am	the	des	qu'est-ce
find	what	je	te
go	when	le	vais
I	you	quand	voir
of			

Words to Know
La boîte à mots

cry
pleure

dark
noir

hide
cache

mom
maman

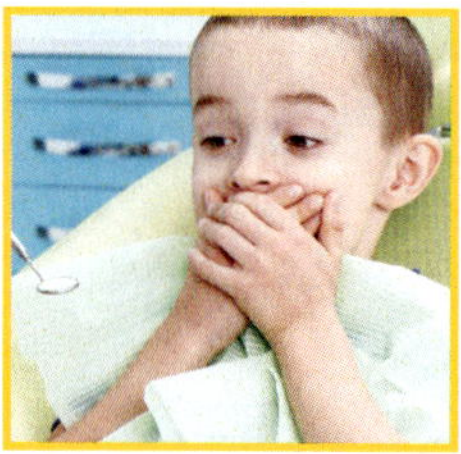

scares
peur

storms
orages

38 Words

What **scares** you?
I am scared of the **dark**.
I **hide** when I am scared.
I am scared of **storms**.
I **cry** when I am scared.
I go find my **mom** when I am scared.
What scares you?

37 mots

Qu'est-ce qui te fait **peur**?
J'ai peur dans le **noir**.
Je me **cache** quand j'ai peur.
J'ai peur des **orages**.
Je **pleure** quand j'ai peur.
Je vais voir **maman** quand j'ai peur.
Qu'est-ce qui te fait peur?

My Emotions

SCARED

Mes émotions

LA PEUR

Written by/Autrice: Amy Culliford
Designed by/Conception: Rhea Wallace
Series Development/Développement des séries: James Earley
Proofreader/Relectrice:: Ellen Rodger
Educational Consultant/Conseillère pédagogique: Marie Lemke M.Ed.
Translated by/Traduction: Annie Evearts

Photographs/Photographies: Shutterstock: Juan Pablo Gonzaález: cover; TY IIm: p. 1; Aleksandr Rybalko: p. 3, 14; Kryzhov: p. 5, 14; justoomm: p. 7, 14; HelloRF Zcool: p. 8, 14; fizkes: p. 9, 14; Inna Ska: p. 13

Crabtree Publishing

crabtreebooks.com 800-387-7650

Published in Canada
Publié au Canada
Crabtree Publishing
616 Welland Ave.
St. Catharines, Ontario
L2M 5V6

Published in the United States
Publié aux États-Unis
Crabtree Publishing
347 Fifth Avenue,
Suite 1402-145
New York, NY, 10016

Paperback 978-1-0398-5099-6
Ebook (pdf) 978-1-0398-5141-2
Epub 978-1-0398-5183-2

Printed in Canada/082024/CP20240812

Library and Archives Canada Cataloguing in Publication
Available at the Library and Archives Canada

Library of Congress Cataloging-in-Publication Data
Available at the Library of Congress